BEE DANCE

Rick
Chrustowski

Henry Holt and Company
New York

When sunlight warms
your honeybee wings,
off you go on flower patrol!

Follow a sweet scent floating on air
to find a honeybee gold mine . . .

. . . a prairie in bloom!

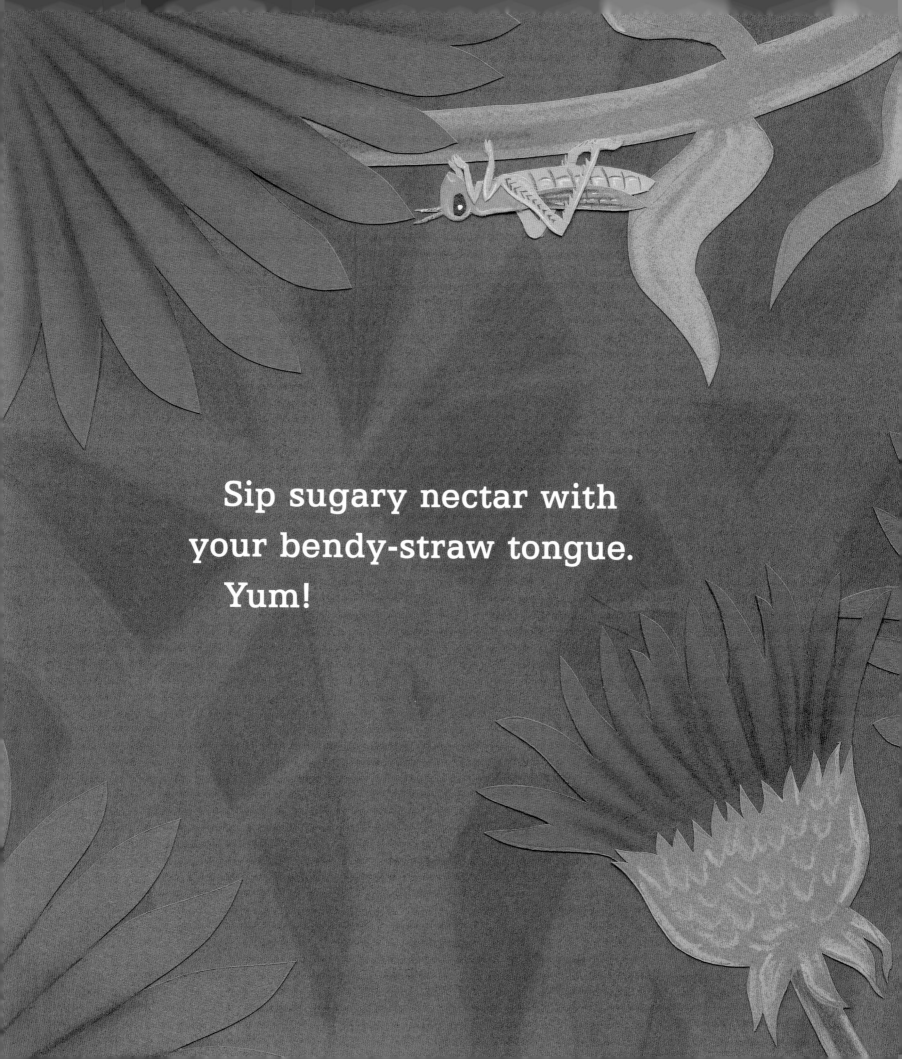

Sip sugary nectar with
your bendy-straw tongue.
Yum!

Race home!

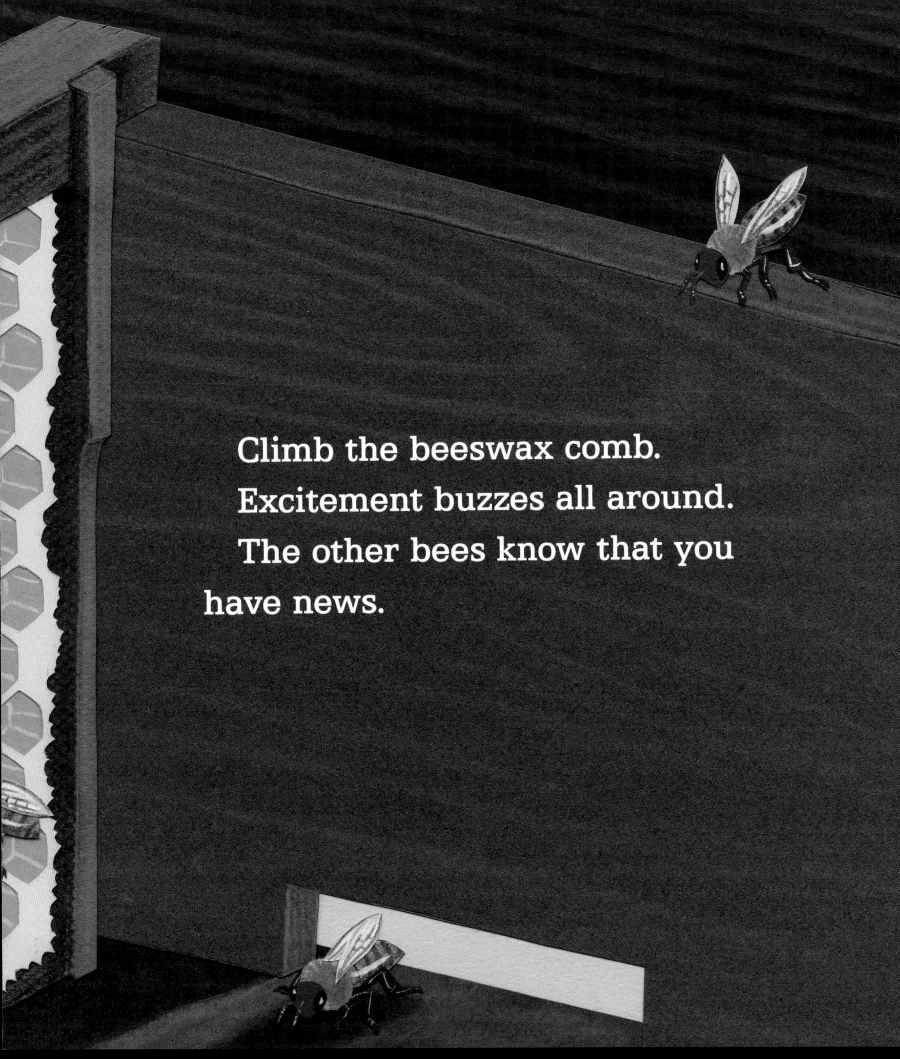

Climb the beeswax comb.
Excitement buzzes all around.
The other bees know that you
have news.

Do the waggle dance, honeybee!
Make a figure eight.
Twirl in a circle.
Wag your body up the
middle run.
Then twirl around the other side.
Buzzz! Buzzz! Buzzz!

Waggle faster, honeybee!
Buzz louder!
Your dance points the way to the prairie.
How long you waggle your body
tells the others how far to go.

Now the bees know just where to fly.

Soon they see flowers
reaching toward the sky.

Go to work, forager bees!
Collect nectar to make
honey.
Stuff pollen into baskets on
your hind legs.

Stay out late.

Carry your heavy prize
back to the hive.
The last glow of sunset
lights the way home.

Unload your cargo and store
it in the combs, then settle in
for the night.

Unload your cargo and store it in the combs, then settle in for the night.

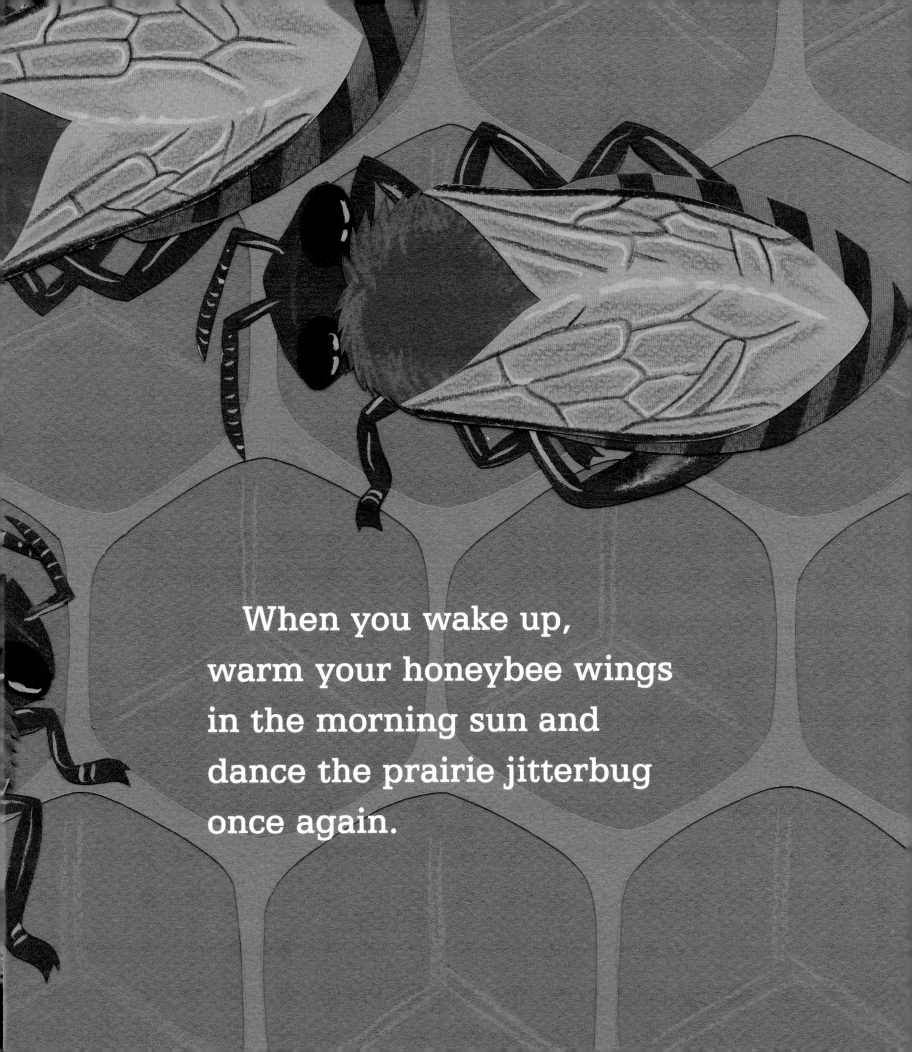

When you wake up,
warm your honeybee wings
in the morning sun and
dance the prairie jitterbug
once again.

Why do honeybees dance?

Honeybees have an amazing way to communicate with one another that is unique in the animal world. They perform a dance that indicates the direction and distance to a rich food source.

When a scout honeybee finds a good batch of flowers, she zips back to the hive to tell the other forager bees where she found it. She climbs the beeswax comb inside the hive, then dances in a figure-eight motion. The waggle run, the straight part between the two circles, shows the angle the food lies relative to the sun's direction. If her waggle run moves up the comb, she is telling them to fly toward the sun in the direction of the angle. If the waggle run moves down the comb, the other bees know to fly away from the sun.

The dancing bee can tell the other bees exactly how far to fly by how long she waggles her body. Each second of waggling stands for a particular distance. For example, if one second of waggling equals 3,000 feet, and the bee waggles her body for 5 seconds in the waggle run, she is telling the forager bees to fly 15,000 feet (or just under three miles) away from the hive.

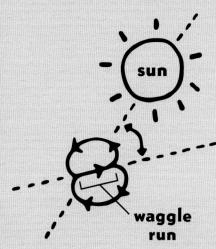
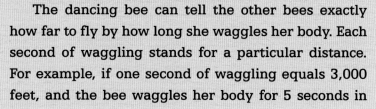

sun

waggle run

During the dance, the bee will pause and give samples of the nectar she gathered to the other bees. They can also "smell" with their antennae the sweet scent of flowers she visited on her body. If the dancing bee buzzes loudly and performs the dance vigorously, the other bees become excited too. They know it is a particularly rich food source, like a prairie in full bloom.

Even though there can be up to 50,000 bees in a hive, it is an orderly place. Each bee has a specific task to perform. There is one queen. She lays the eggs. There are thousands of worker bees. They care for young bees, clean and guard the hive, build the combs, scout for new food sources, and forage for nectar and pollen. At certain times of year, drones, or male bees, are produced to mate with queens from other hives.

For Laura Godwin, her beekeeper father, and all beekeepers around the world

Special thanks to Dr. Thomas Seeley, Professor of Neurobiology and Behavior at Cornell University, for vetting this text and the illustrations. Read his book *Honeybee Democracy* to learn more about the fascinating topic of swarm intelligence.

Henry Holt and Company, LLC
Publishers since 1866
120 Broadway, New York, NY 10271
mackids.com

Library of Congress Cataloging-in-Publication Data
Chrustowski, Rick, author, illustrator.
Bee dance / Rick Chrustowski. — First edition.
   pages   cm
Audience: Ages 4–8.
ISBN 978-0-8050-9919-5
1. Honeybee—Behavior—Juvenile literature. 2. Worker honeybees—Juvenile literature. 3. Animal communication—Juvenile literature. I. Title.
QL568.A6C47 2015   595.79'9159—dc23   2014028619

Henry Holt books may be purchased for business or promotional use. For information on bulk purchases, please contact the Macmillan Corporate and Premium Sales Department at (800) 221-7945 x5442 or by e-mail at specialmarkets@macmillan.com.

First Edition—2015/Designed by Ashley Halsey
The illustrations in this book are cut paper collage with pastel pencil details.
Printed in China by RR Donnelley Asia Printing Solutions Ltd., Dongguan City, Guangdong Province

20 19 18 17 16 15 14 13